Create "Aha!" Moments: Tips for Learners

Dennison S. Bhola

Michelle L. Piel

Dedication from Dennison:

This book is dedicated to my mom, Sheila "Biggie" Bhola formerly Dinoo, a lifelong learner who was a teacher for four decades; and to my grandsons, Tahj and Tyce Christian Mumgaard, who I encourage to approach learning with an open mind and apply the tips in this book.

A message to my grandsons:

Create your vision.
    Map out your future,
    set goals, make a plan,
...and work your plan.
    Be flexible, don't fear change.
    When you reach obstacles, find a way over,
    around, or through them.
Your plan will evolve with new insights; transform your vision into reality.
    Be kind to others.
    Stay humble.
    Grow & enjoy the journey.

Dedication from Michelle:

This book is dedicated to you, Lindsey and Amanda, to whom I leave two things, one is roots, the other is wings. I hope you will read this book, strengthen your wings, and become the persons you want to be—soaring at a high enough altitude to see where you are and know where you are headed in life.

Acknowledgements

The authors would like to express our appreciation to those who helped us prepare this book for publishing.

Robyn Hatfield, marketing technology guru. Thanks for helping us launch this book. Your professionalism is top notch.

Salma Kalloo, illustrator. We appreciate your talent and time in creating wonderful line drawings to complement each chapter.

Daniel Neuman, designer. Thanks for transforming our concepts into a cover design that tells the story of what this book is all about.

Valeria Ramdin, senior reviewer. We value the time, ideas, and contributions you provided early in the review process.

Toanya Rahim, senior reviewer. Thank you for looking at an early excerpt through the eyes of a teacher and sharing your perspective.

Lindsey Piel, Amanda Piel, & Tahj Christian Mumgaard, junior reviewers. We appreciate your keen eyes, honesty, and feedback which was positive and constructive. It makes us proud of you to know that you can edit a book so thoroughly and insightfully as students and writers who have withstood a critique or two.

To our readers, we hope you enjoy the stories, illustrations, and tips provided in this book. Please share it with others who may find it helpful.

Sincerely,

Dennison S. Bhola & Michelle L. Piel

Table of Contents

Introduction

How do I choose the path that leads to knowledge, skills, and self-confidence?

This book was created to support you in your quest for knowledge and success. Think of it like an owner's manual for making the best use of your brain. It answers the essential question: "As a student, how can I learn more and remember longer?" Read this book if you want to improve your learning skills.

Every year you have new classes to tackle in school. At times, you might wonder about <u>what</u> you learn. We suggest that <u>how</u> you learn is just as important. Your curiosity and creativity can help you improve your learning skills.

This book focuses on how you can develop into a successful learner.

Book Design: Aha! Moments for Life

The more you learn, the more you grow. Apply what is in this book and you can master each lesson in school and in life. Choose your goal, make a plan with a timeline, work your plan, and success will follow.

This book is intentionally designed to increase your knowledge, skills, and self-confidence. We provide insights into what your teacher is thinking as she prepares a lesson or assignment to help you learn. These insights ensure that you target the most important information first. This is a key. Learn what is most important first and the rest will follow.

Throughout this book, we share stories to illustrate main points and inspire you to take charge of your own learning. As you become an intentional learner, you will create your own vision and exercise your freedom to learn and grow.

The ideas in this book are valuable for learners of all ages. Make use of the ideas that help you the most. You can contact us with questions and suggestions using the contact us form in the createahamoments.com website.

1

What are Aha! Moments?

Aha! Moments are when you can
say, "I get it."

This chapter discusses what you can do to have more "Aha! Moments".

<u>Main Points:</u>

1. What are Aha! Moments?
2. What can Aha! Moments do for me?
3. How can I create more Aha! Moments?

<u>What are Aha! Moments?</u>

You experience an Aha! Moment every time you learn something new. In your brain, during an Aha! Moment your neurons (brain cells) connect new information with what you already know. Aha! Moments are instants when you can say, "I get it!"

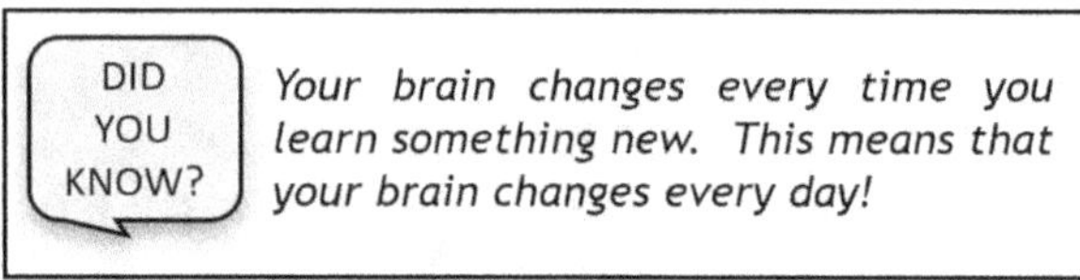

In your neural network, connection points are the places where your neurons weld together. Each time you experience an Aha! Moment, you create new connections.

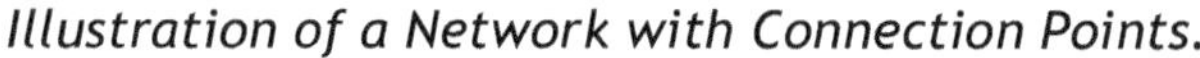

Illustration of a Network with Connection Points.

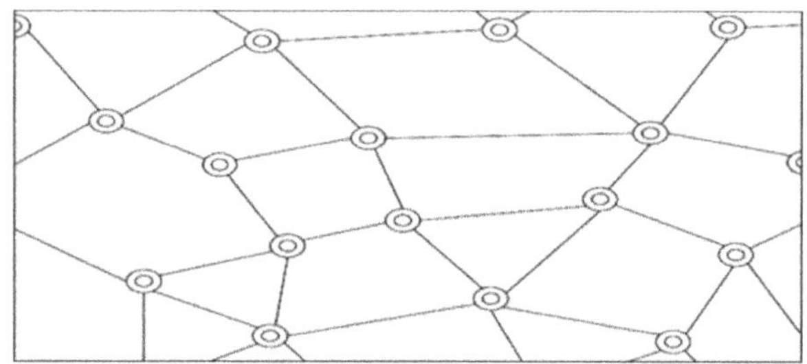

<u>What can Aha! Moments do for you?</u>

Think of what you know like a social network. Each Aha! Moment is like adding a friend to your network. Just as your social network grows when you add new friends, your neural network grows when you learn something new. With every new connection, you experience an Aha! Moment.

A network shows how things are connected to each other. In a social network, friends are connected. In your brain's network, your neurons are connected.

The Value of Practice

Messages travel along the connections between your neurons. The more frequently you use these connections, the stronger they become. Just like chatting with a friend strengthens your relationship, recalling what you learn strengthens your memories.

Applying what you learn makes the relevant parts of your brain work together. The more you practice what you have learned, the stronger the connections become. Stronger connections mean that you can remember what you learn for longer periods of time.

How can I create more Aha! Moments?

For strong connections to be made in your brain, you need to recall and use what you have learned. Think of this activity like giving your neural connections some mental exercise. You are in charge of coaching your brain through the workout.

Here is an example of a basic plan that will exercise your ability to create more Aha! Moments:

Daily Workout for Learning

1. Tune in.
2. Participate.
3. Master the lesson.

Tune In

Attention is the first step. To have more Aha! Moments, listen and focus on finding out the most important points of the lesson. Ask yourself, "What are the main points?"

Knowing the main points help you pay attention intelligently. Use them to stay tuned in and make it more likely that you will remember what you learn.

Participate

Be an active learner. Participate in your daily education. To obtain the greatest benefit from class, take notes, ask questions, show your work, and help others learn. Attack the "workouts" that your teacher provides. Break a sweat with your thoughts. Seriously, mental effort strengthens your neural network.

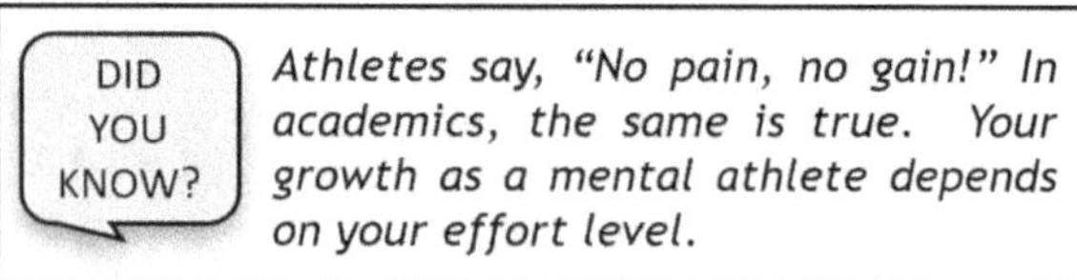

<u>Master the Lesson</u>

Set a goal to master every lesson. To ensure mastery, take time to reflect on what you learn. Each day, ask yourself whether or not you can recall, explain, and apply what you learned. Take stock of what you know and what you do not know.

Quick Tips for Mastering a Lesson

> Step 1 – Recall What You Learned
> - Try to identify the main points from memory.
> - What do you remember best and least?
>
> Step 2 – Review Your Notes
> - Did you cover all of the main points?
> - Review the examples given in class and fill in any information gaps.

Review what you learned by using your brainpower every day. Be sure that you can explain and apply what you learned in the lesson. Start with a solid fifteen minute review and extend your brain workout over time. Just as physical activities at the gym strengthen your muscles, consistent mental workouts strengthen your learning skills. Savor your Aha! Moments as you review, master each lesson, and grow.

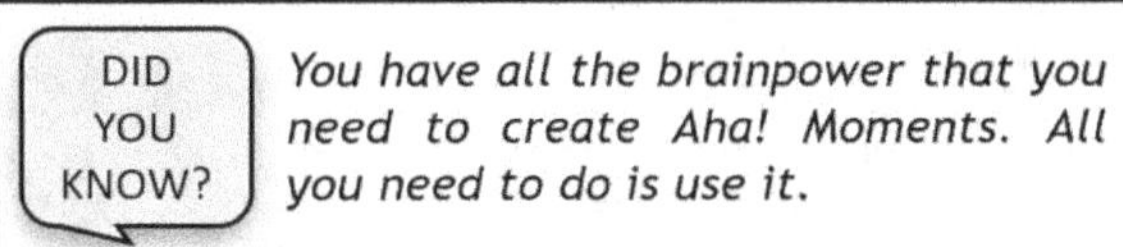

Chapter 1 - Summary

Aha! Moments are instants in which learning occurs. Just like you would add a new friend to your social network, learning adds new knowledge to your neural network.

Applying your new learning makes different parts of your brain work together. When this happens, you increase the "friends" in your neural network and strengthen the connections between them.

To create more Aha! moments for yourself, pay attention in class and invest sufficient effort to master the lesson. Participate by asking good questions, taking notes, and showing your work. Exercise your mind with a thorough review of the main points. Ask, "What did I learn? How do I apply what I learned?" Workout your brain to master each lesson.

"We are what we repeatedly do. Excellence, then, is not an act but a habit." – Will Durant

In the next chapter we discuss how you can work with your teacher to transform errors into "Aha! Moments".

2

The Value of a Guide

"What you can do today with assistance, you will be able to do by yourself tomorrow." - Lev Vygotski

This chapter discusses the value of having a "guide" on your learning journey. Imagine that you are an explorer on an expedition to climb Mount Everest. You examine maps of the terrain and hire a Sherpa, a local guide. Your guide has lived in the Himalayas all his life. Having made the trip many times, he knows how to get you to the top. Just as explorers need guides, learners need teachers.

<u>Main Points:</u>

1. What is guided practice?
2. Why does your teacher need to see your work?
3. How is guided practice good for you?

<u>Why is practice important?</u>

You may have heard that "practice makes perfect", but have you heard that "practice makes permanent." To consistently perform with excellence, learners need to practice correct skills and reasoning.

When you are learning something new it is hard to know whether you are making errors. This is exactly when having a guide to observe your work and provide feedback helps you the most.

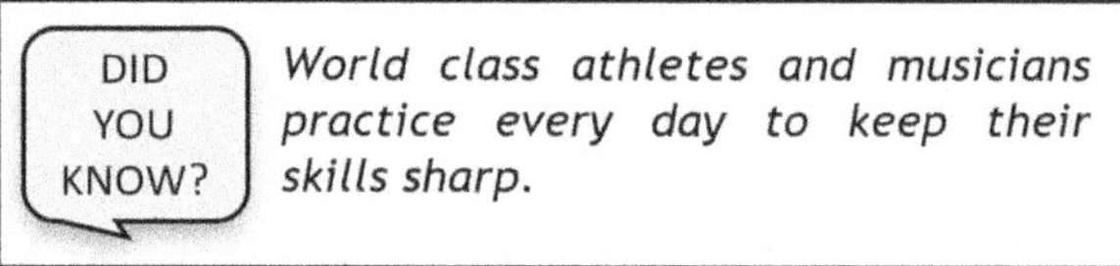

<u>What is guided practice?</u>

In the classroom, your teacher is the guide. Outside of school, knowledgeable people can serve as guides for your learning. In this chapter, we are going to focus on guided practice inside of school.

Teachers prepare guided practice activities to ensure you understood what they taught in the lesson. In school, your teacher provides guided practice when she gives you a question and observes your reasoning and skills. During practice, your teacher may notice a few things that you do not understand.

By observing your work, your teacher can diagnose why you are making certain errors. After posing a few questions and listening to your ideas, she will provide valuable tips to help you master the lesson. Isn't it great to have a "guide by your side" until you can do the work independently?

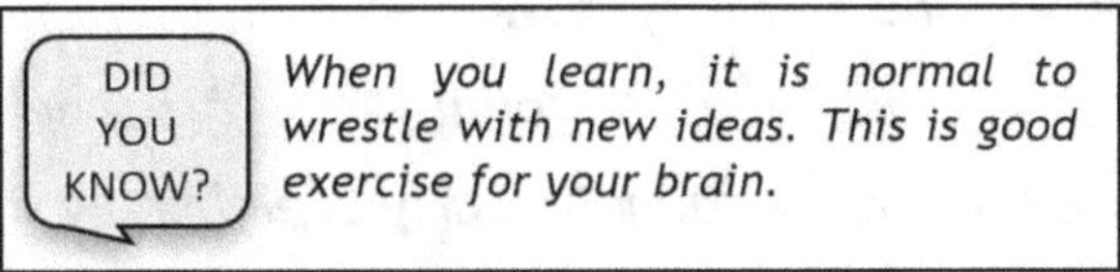

A Story: What guided practice is not!

Let's say that you learned a math concept. The teacher ran out of time to assign practice problems to do in class. Instead, she assigned ten questions for homework. When you get home, the first three solutions are straightforward.

Then, you get stuck on a question because the directions seem unclear. You realize that you are missing vital information to complete the homework. When you cannot understand the directions, what can you do about it?

You want to finish the assignment. This afternoon you downloaded a new game on your tablet before Mom reminded you: "No screen time until you finish the math assignment."

Maybe this is one of those times to ask Mom for help? She is still pretty smart even though she went to school twenty years ago. You barely remember the last time you asked her for help. That time, she started reading your math book to figure out what you were supposed to do. Oh well, nothing to lose!

You ask Mom. She works on solving the problem for ten minutes. This includes her coming up with the right answer even though she cannot clearly explain how she did it. She does not solve the equation with the same process that your teacher uses in class.

Mom is pleased and tries to explain what she did. Her explanation is confusing because it is not how your teacher would say it. This is not helping. Not only do you miss playing your new game, you cannot correctly answer all of the homework questions.

<u>What happened here?</u>

The teacher assigned homework without any in-class practice time for you to apply what you learned during the lesson. So, you did not have an opportunity to practice, make errors, and receive feedback from your teacher. When you miss out on guided practice, you may leave class with faulty ideas and without the information you need to complete your homework.

If this happens to you, it is OK to reach out to your teacher at a reasonable hour outside of school. Contact your teacher in the way that he or she prefers (e.g., phone, email, text).

<u>What if we could turn back the clock?</u>
Ideally, the teacher provided a step-by-step demonstration of how to use the information to answer questions like those assigned for homework. While you were still in class, she gave you an opportunity to work a sample problem all the way through to a final answer. The teacher observed how individual students tackled the work in class. She helped your friend figure out a multiplication error.

When you got confused, she noticed. She came alongside you and explained the task using simple words. She watched you work on solving the problem. She asked questions so that you could describe your reasoning. Then, she described the correct reasoning for you to compare with your own.

Aha! You saw the first path that you took and how it was different from the final path leading to the solution. Your teacher offered a reminder on how to approach that type of problem in the future.

Then, she gave you a similar question. You tried it and the correct reasoning for all of the steps made sense to you. You felt happy to show your step-by-step solution to your teacher. She nodded and smiled with satisfaction as she gave you another question. You solved it correctly on the first try. You felt the glow of an Aha! Moment!

<u>What was different this time?</u>

Your teacher observed your work and she explained the directions in simple language. You left class with skills and confidence. When you tackled your homework, you had success.

<u>How is guided practice good for you?</u>

Guided practice can help you master the correct reasoning. During guided practice, mistakes are not allowed to take root. Your teacher uses your errors to help you correct your reasoning.

Once you have mastered the lesson, doing your homework strengthens your memories for the correct reasoning.

When you go to sleep at night, your brain saves the reasoning that you believe is correct. And, this is what you remember in the future.

Chapter 2 - Summary

Teachers use guided practice to ensure that you understand the lesson and can apply correct reasoning. Well-made guided practice activities reveal what you know and where you need help.

Guided practice gives you time to "practice" what you just learned under your teacher's watchful eyes. Let your teacher observe your work. When something does not make sense, ask for help. She can provide explanations to help you learn. In these moments, you will enjoy having a "guide by your side".

During guided practice, your teacher observes your work and helps you to master the correct reasoning and skills. Having a guide who you can ask for help is what makes guided practice different from "unguided" practice. Once you "get it" you are ready for homework. Practicing what you learn strengthens your memory of the lesson.

In the next chapter, we discuss useful feedback and how it can improve your performance.

3

Apply Useful Feedback

You will know feedback is useful
because you stop making errors.

This chapter describes how to ask for useful feedback when you need it.

<u>Main Points:</u>

1. What is useful feedback?
2. How does useful feedback help you learn?
3. Why do you need to see the "gap"?

In the last chapter, we described the value of having a <u>guide</u> during guided practice. A key benefit is that your guide provides useful feedback.

<u>What is useful feedback?</u>

Useful feedback describes what to do and what not to do. Once you see the correct path, you can navigate from where you are on your learning journey to where you need to finish. In this way, feedback creates "Aha! Moments" for you.

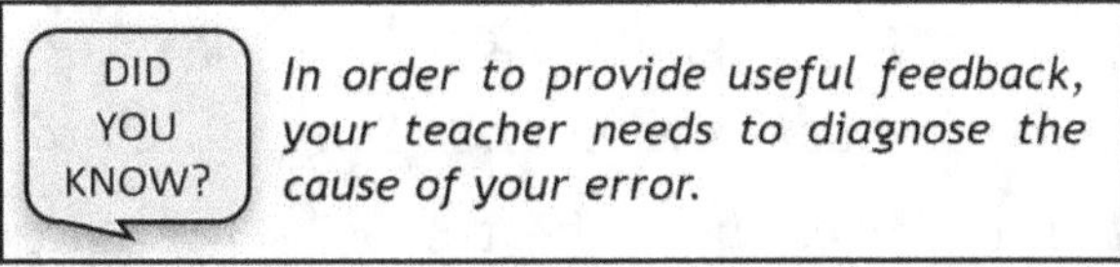

When you learn something new, things may not go right at first. To request feedback from your teacher: ask questions, show your work, and explain where you are stuck. Your teacher will diagnose the cause of the errors and share specific actions that you can take to close the "gap".

<u>Feedback Story: Chef J. helps Sandy</u>

Sandy loves to cook. She enjoys cooking shows where experts critique the finished product. Sandy and her friends like to pretend they have their own cooking show in Mom's kitchen. Using basic ingredients found in the pantry, they compete to see who can make the best treats in thirty minutes. A parent or friend plays along as their judge. After the judge's critiques, the group enjoys taste testing their snacks.

Sandy likes to cook for her family and hear their reviews. Dad usually compliments her on everything she makes. Her sister Mindy is her harshest critic. Mom lets Sandy cook whatever and whenever, but she reminds Sandy, "Please clean up after you are done making a mess in my kitchen!"

Sandy keeps a notebook of her favorite recipes. A quick review of her notebook reveals that Sandy loves to bake. One night she bakes her "best-ever" chocolate chip cookies. Although the cookies did not turn out as well as last time, her first bite proves that the cookies are good enough to share. Sandy offers her family members a nice warm cookie to try.

Mom says, "Something is missing. Did you clean up the kitchen yet?"

Dad says, "Thanks, these are delicious! Mm-mm so good."

Mindy says, "You forgot salt. I like salt and there's no salt in these cookies."

Sandy smiles. She just got feedback from her personal panel of food critics! Mom, Dad, and Mindy are steady customers, but they are not real good bakers. Sandy needs better feedback to improve her baking skills. As usual, her family members are only giving their opinions.

Sandy wants to improve her cookies. After cleaning the kitchen, she reviews her notebook. The recipe clearly lists salt as the ninth ingredient. As Sandy reflects, she wonders how her baking skills stack up to those of a professional. If she knew what great cooks do, then she could close the gap.

Sandy wants to make great tasting cookies every time. She realizes that it is not just the cookies that need improvement. Sandy needs to improve her cooking skills.

<u>How could an instructor help Sandy?</u>

A qualified instructor would know how to give helpful feedback based on cooking expertise and teaching experience. Instructors can review learners' skills and explain why certain steps are necessary. Instructors observe learners in action and provide useful feedback.

<u>Sandy's Story (continued)</u>

Sandy needs an instructor. She searches "cookie baking courses" online and clicks on one she likes. The course is called "Baking Basics". She like this because it promises:

1. *Step-by-step instructions with tips from a master chef.*
2. *Observation and feedback.*
3. *Consistently delicious results.*

Mom reads about the course and agrees to pay for the lessons. She likes the idea of Sandy baking in the Chef's kitchen. She sees the value of Sandy making cookies under the watchful eyes of an expert who can provide useful feedback. Mom hopes that as Sandy improves, she will not waste so much of the sugar and flour in the pantry.

Before going to sleep, Sandy considers what her family said about the cookies. Mom was vague; Dad offered praise; and Mindy told her what she did wrong. None of this feedback helped Sandy improve her baking skills. She tries not to take the criticism to heart.

<u>Why does Sandy need to see the "gap"?</u>

Hearing that she has done something "right" or "wrong" is not enough information to help Sandy improve her skills. For feedback to be considered "useful," she needs to understand what to do and why.

<u>Sandy's Story (Continued)</u>

Fortunately, the next day Sandy begins one-on-one "Baking Basics" with Chef J. After Sandy describes her dilemma, Chef J. says, "Let's go into the kitchen and see how I can be helpful to you."

Next, Chef J. shows Sandy what to do to get delicious results. She lets Sandy make cookies in her "test" kitchen. Chef J. observes an error. Sandy is running around as if she is on a cooking show, retrieving one item then adding it to the bowl, then going to get something else, grabbing two or three ingredients here and there. Pow! Sandy tosses ingredients into the bowl with so much flair! Clearly, Sandy enjoys the glamour of adding ingredients and mixing up the dough. Because of the movement and chaos, Sandy could easily miss adding one or more of the proper ingredients. Surely, Sandy must know that the recipe requires each ingredient to turn out perfect.

Chef J. says, "Sandy, it is important to gather all of your ingredients before you start mixing them."

"OK. I did that, kinda."

"OK Sandy did you line them up in the order that they would be used?"

"Oops. No, I did not do that. Hmmm. How does that help?"

"Sandy there is a convention that chefs everywhere follow. Cooking is a version of storytelling. Like a story, recipes are passed along and follow a certain order. It is important to know that good recipes list ingredients in the exact order that they will be added from start to finish. Chefs follow the step-by-step recipe instructions. To get great results every time, line up your ingredients to match the listed order and recipe instructions. This is what great cooks and chefs consistently do."

The lightbulb goes on for Sandy. "Oh, I get it! I can do that." Sandy has her "Aha! Moment". She's glad her mom *signed her up for "Baking Basics". Chef J. is so helpful. And, just like at home, Sandy has to clean up the mess she made before leaving the kitchen.*

Chef J. summarizes the lesson, "Sandy, the next time you make anything, remember to line up all of the ingredients in the order that you plan to use them. Then, you can focus on adding each ingredient as you follow the instructions. I'm excited to see your notebook. Next time we meet, let's go over recipe writing so you can add well written recipes to your notebook."

Sandy smiles broadly. She plans to practice her favorite chocolate chip cookie recipe again as soon as she gets home. She feels confident about asking Mindy to try the next cookie.

<u>How can your teacher help you close the gap?</u>
When your teacher provides useful feedback, she helps you compare your steps with the correct steps. Then, you will see the "gap". With your teacher's help, you can learn how to correct your errors and close the "gap".

Your goal is to use the feedback to improve. Listen and find out what to do differently. Once you understand what to do, apply the feedback and master the lesson.

Mastery requires consistent practice. For the correct information to stick in your memory, accuracy is required. Perfect practice makes perfect performance.

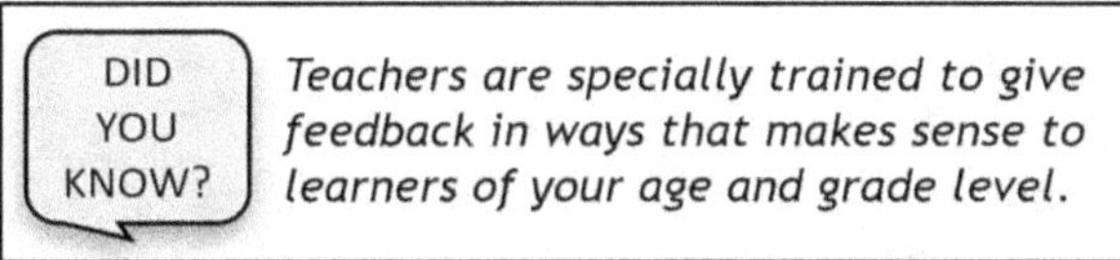

Imagine Life Without Feedback

We would have to figure things out on our own. We might think our reasoning is correct when it is faulty. This is a shaky foundation for learning.

When you make errors, isn't it nice to know your teacher cares enough to provide useful feedback? Your teachers believe in your ability or they would not share honest feedback. Listen, keep an open mind, and strive for improvement.

Chapter 3 - Summary

Useful feedback includes clear explanations and relevant examples. It is one of the best tools for mastering a lesson. It helps you see the steps you need to take to close any learning gaps.

If you detect an error, try to close the gap using what you know. If you cannot close the gap on your own, then ask your teacher for help. Your teacher can provide useful feedback.

Your teacher's main goal is to ensure that you master the correct reasoning and skills. She can provide step-by-step explanations to allow you to compare your steps with the correct steps. You need to "see" the gap to close the gap. Pay close attention to the feedback. Then, put the tips into practice.

In the next chapter, we share pointers for staying awake in class.

Manage Your Attention Level

Your attention level changes like a
rollercoaster. What can you do to
manage it?

In class, the clock is always ticking. Has your attention
ever wandered in the middle of a lecture?

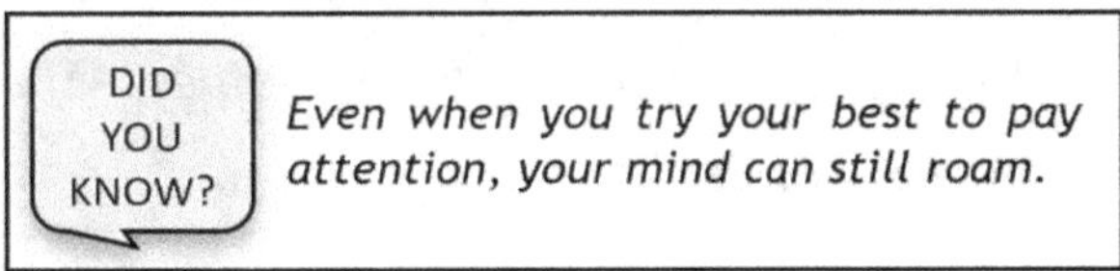

This chapter shares what you can do to stay alert in class.

Main Points:

1. When do you have to fight the hardest to pay
    attention?

2. What is down-time?

3. How can you stay alert?

Learning requires brainwork and energy. When your brain is busy learning it connects incoming information with what you already know. Naturally, parts of the brain become tired if you use them nonstop for a while. When parts of your brain get tired, attention fades. Our next story illustrates how attention affects learning.

<u>A Story: The Great Dust Bowl</u>

Mindy could see herself cycling down Fairview Avenue. Her tabby cat sat inside a colorful bike basket. Maybe she was going a bit too fast. The cat's eyes opened wide as Mindy rounded a curve. The bike skidded, a whirl of dust blew up, and kitty flew out of the basket.

"Meow! M-e-o-w-y?" she heard.

A familiar voice spoke to her. "M-i-n-d-y," the teacher said firmly. Uh-oh, busted! Mindy sat up straight. A jolt of reality went up the middle of her spine. She had daydreamed in class again.

"Mindy, please pay attention."

"Yes, sorry ma'am." Mindy nodded and picked up her pencil as if to make a note.

Her teacher went back to teaching. She covered the third cause of the Great Dust Bowl. She directed the class: "Within the next five minutes, summarize the three main causes of the Dust Bowl? Then, hand me your papers when the bell rings."

Mindy's heart sank. Although technically Mindy did not fall asleep, her mind had drifted away from the teacher's voice. She had a problem. She could only recall the first and last causes of the Dust Bowl from her notes. She must have missed the <u>middle</u> one while she was "riding her bike with Fluffy." Oh well, at least Fluffy was OK. Mindy chuckled.

Her teacher hovered over her asking softly, "Mindy, what is so funny? I think you should stay in for lunch and we can figure out what you missed."

<u>What happens in the middle of a lecture?</u>

Have you ever noticed that your attention dips during the middle of a lesson? Your attention level affects how much you learn. If your attention is not focused on learning, you will miss important information just like Mindy did.

Your attention level naturally changes during a lecture. The following graph shows how your attention can go up and down like a rollercoaster.

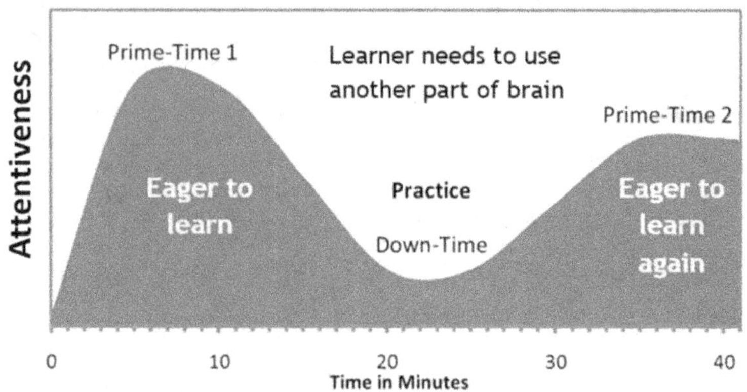

In the "U" shaped attention curve, the high points are called "prime-times" and the dip is "down-time". "Prime-time-1" is the peak period of attention at the start of the lesson. "Prime-time 2" is the peak at the end. An area of "down-time" occurs in the middle. Just like Mindy during the Dust Bowl lesson, when you sit in class your attention can fade.

The middle of this "U" shaped curve is cause for concern for teachers and students everywhere! Actual learning happens when your brain is attentive. Managing your attention level impacts how much you will remember. You do not want to daydream in the middle of class. Now you know why!

Falling asleep during a lecture or movie is most likely to occur during down-time. When you doze off, your attention and ability to remember the lesson drop to zero.

The Story of the "Sleepy" Cadets

At the United States Air Force Academy, cadets never rest. Outside of class, they participate in athletics, study, march, do inspections, attend football games, and fulfill military duties on campus. Most cadets do not get much sleep.

Even though cadets are top students, they tend to nod off during class. To combat downtime, the Academy allows cadets to stand at the back of the classroom. Most cadets do not want to risk falling asleep on their feet and tipping over like a teapot. When this happens, classmates are entertained, but the instructor is not too amused.

How can I stay alert?

First, staying alert in school is a matter of getting enough rest. Try setting an alarm to remind yourself to go to bed just like you do to get up in the morning. If you feel sleepy in class, ask your teacher for permission to stand up and take notes. This will help you stay more alert than sitting. The bottom line is when you feel "drowsy" at your desk, standing up is better for your circulation.

As you might suspect, blood circulation affects your ability to think and pay attention. Have you ever fallen asleep when you are on a long road trip? Interestingly, after humans sit still for twenty minutes, about twenty percent of their blood pools in the big muscles of the quads, hamstrings, and buttocks.

To get your blood back into circulation for "thinking and learning," consider moving around from time to time. Even a simple, thirty-second break in which you stand, stretch, and sit again helps your circulation. This makes more oxygen available to your brain and re-energizes you.

<u>What else can I do to stay alert?</u>
In school, you are expected to stay seated most of the time so prepare to manage your attention level with that in mind. After mostly listening and watching your teacher present information for twenty minutes or more, your brain tires of working in "recorder-mode". When your teacher lectures into down-time, you need to act like a "reporter" chasing a news story.

Be a reporter, not a recorder. To remain alert, imagine you need to capture vital information for a news story. Ask questions and listen for clues to explain what's happening in the lesson. Create questions and capture the main points for retelling.

Use your curiosity. Think: What do I need to know? Why? Posing questions helps your brain focus on the main points of the lesson.

"Why?" and "How?"

Wanting to learn "why" and "how" compels you to listen, think, and probe for answers. Reporters are driven by this kind of thinking. Your role as a learner can be fueled by this too. Thinking like a reporter can help you target the main points during a lecture.

For example, if Mindy thought like a reporter, at the start of her notes she would have written: 'Why did the Dust Bowl happen?' and, 'How did people handle this crisis?' and, 'How did this change farming?'. Then, by listening for the answers to these questions she could have nailed the main points of the lesson.

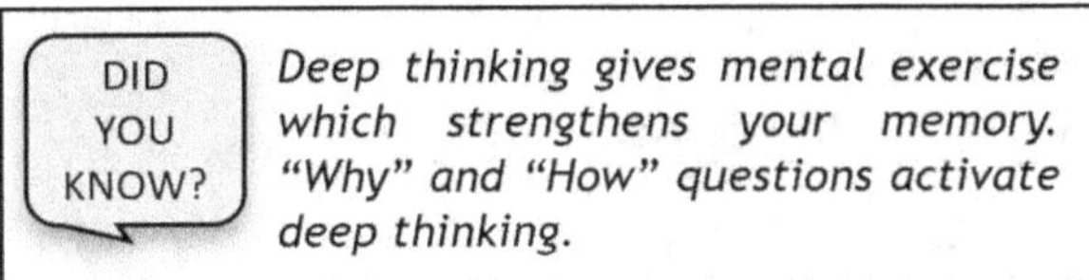

As you listen for answers to your questions, you may need to pose a question to your teacher. A good question helps you explore your observations and gain relevant information from the expert.

<u>More Tips</u>

During class, take notes that highlight the main points of the lesson. When you review your notes later, you will be able to identify key ideas and remember the lesson as you "read" the story.

Tips for staying alert as you take notes:
1. Use capital letters or icons for key words.
2. Make pictures with captions that will remind you of the main points.
3. Create an advertisement for the lesson.

In class, practice your ability to stay alert and attentive. In your seat, sit up nice and straight. Breathe quietly down into your belly for maximum oxygen. As you do these activities, make sure that you pay attention to the lesson and do not distract those around you. Be considerate of others and do not disrupt class.

<u>How do teachers help you stay attentive?</u>

Teachers intentionally switch the "Learning Channel" and prompt students to speak, think, or do something. Teachers can ask you to share your ideas. Discussions give your voice some airtime. Hearing the sound of your own voice is helpful for learning.

When you are asked to come up with answers during a "Think-Pair-Share" activity, you get to think for a couple minutes, and then discuss answers with a partner before sharing your thoughts with the rest of the class. Your active participation squashes down-time. To keep your brain alert, cooperate when your teacher strives to:

1. Reenergize your brain with a stand up and stretch break.
2. Initiate a question and answer period.
3. Provide guided practice in-class for you to apply what you have just learned.
4. Play learning games (e.g., Jeopardy) that raise your knowledge and energy levels.

Take advantage of these refreshing changes and keep your brain "on task".

Chapter 4 – Summary

Attention is the first step in learning. How closely you pay attention is under your control.

Prime-time and down-time explain how attention levels naturally change during a lecture. At the beginning and end of a lesson your brain is eager to learn. Take advantage of your alertness during prime-time to capture the main points.

In the middle of a lecture down-time naturally occurs. During downtime, do what you can to stay alert rather than let your attentiveness drop. Like a reporter, ask "why" and "how" questions that keep you focused on the main points. Make well-written notes to review later.

In the next chapter we provide tips you can use to strengthen your memory.

5

Remember the Lesson

To remember what you learn,
summarize and review.

This chapter describes what you can do to remember a lesson today, tomorrow, and for the future.

Main Points:

1. What happens in my brain while I sleep?
2. When should I summarize the main points of a lesson?
3. Why review? How do I review?

<u>Why is it good to remember what you learn?</u>
To grow, we must remember the lessons we learn and build upon them. Each day we add "friends" to our neural network and save these "connections". As learners, we

need to build our base of knowledge and skills over time. That's how expertise develops.

Just imagine that you want to become a doctor. In seventh grade, learning about the muscles, bones, and nervous system becomes knowledge that you can use and build upon for your future career. Even if you do not want to become a doctor, you can apply knowledge about the human body to stay healthy and understand conversations with your doctor.

Knowledge flows from one lesson to another. To retain what you learn, summarize and review often; and, get enough sleep!

<u>What happens in my brain while I sleep?</u>
During sleep, your brain stores information that you view as important, useful, and personally relevant to make memories. These memories are what you can recall 24 hours or more after the lesson. Make note of the main points from the lesson. This way your brain knows what to save while you sleep.

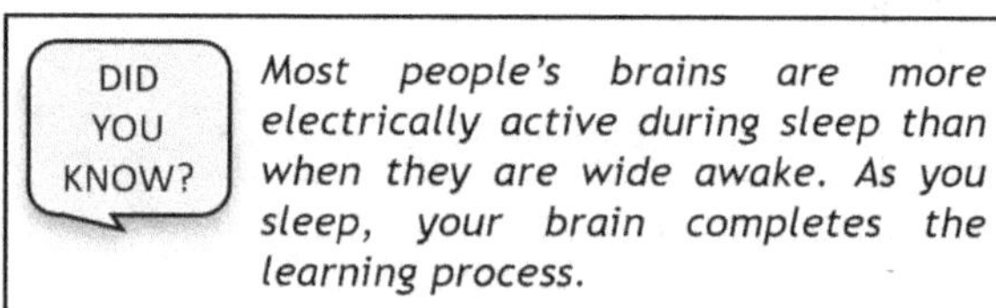

<u>When should I summarize the main points of a lesson?</u>

View the end of a lesson like the end of a game and play with extra intensity in the final minutes. At the end of every lesson, spend about five minutes reminding yourself of the main points. Instead of thinking about lunch or your next class, make it a habit to summarize what you learned. Keep in mind that five minutes invested while you are in class could save you hours later.

The sooner you summarize, the easier the lesson is to recall. The longer you delay, the more the information slips away. It is easiest to remember a lesson while you are still in class. And, if you have questions you can ask your teacher for information.

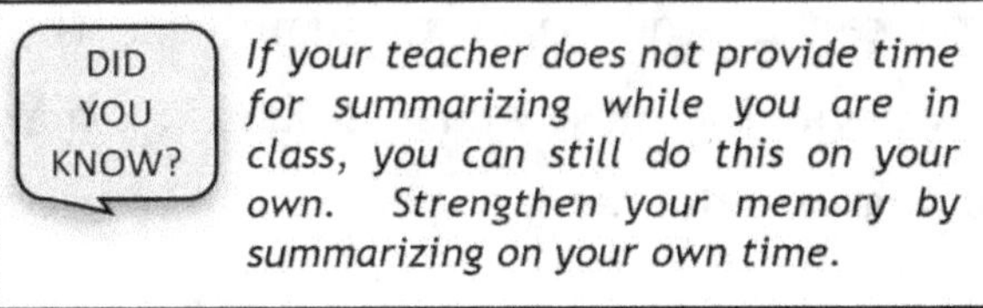

If your teacher does not provide time for summarizing while you are in class, you can still do this on your own. Strengthen your memory by summarizing on your own time.

If you cannot summarize the main points of the lesson before you leave class, please do so as soon as possible. Summarization is important. It helps your brain know what information to save for future use. Make sure that you summarize your lessons at some point before you go to sleep.

<u>What do I need to do when I summarize?</u>

When you summarize, clarify what your brain needs to remember the most. Tell your brain what to remember. For instance, fill in these blanks with information: Today's "math" lesson was about "_________".

Summarizing a lesson is a good habit because it strengthens your memories. Mark or highlight the most important points and key words in your notes. Make check boxes next to ideas you want to go over later, as if to say to your brain, "Here is what I need to clarify!" Each time you review the information later, check the boxes. This keeps a tally of the number of times you reviewed the information.

Just like you can use questions to help you pay attention in class, you can use questions to summarize the main points of a lesson. The most valuable questions make you think about what you learned.

Ask yourself "how" and "why" questions to help you think deeply about the main points of the lesson. Put on your learning detective hat and seek answers to your questions. Ensure the answers you find are correct. If you are unsure, discuss them with your teacher.

<u>"Sleep on it."</u>

While you sleep, your brain completes a mental process to save memories of your daily lessons. You need about eight hours of sleep to complete this process properly. Depriving your brain of sleep is not good for learning. Follow a routine that balances your need for study time with your need for sleep.

In order to get enough sleep, you need to manage your time wisely. Set an alarm to remind yourself of when to go to bed. If you wake up at 6am, this means that you need to be asleep by 10pm. In order to give your brain enough time to complete the memory-making process, you need to get sufficient rest.

One of the best habits for memory making is to summarize the lesson in class, or certainly before you go to sleep, and then "sleep on it".

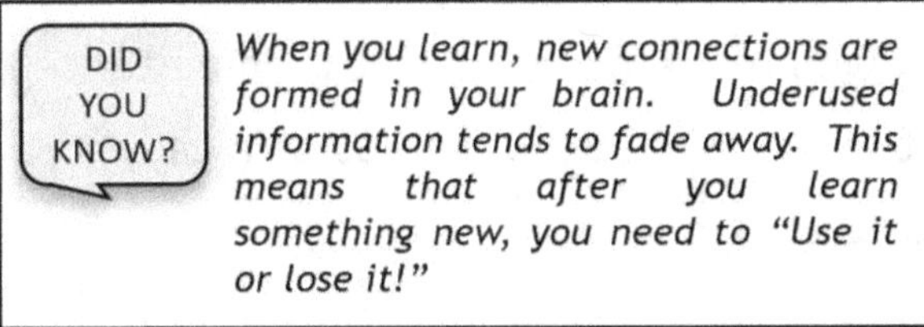

So, the next question you may ask is: "Let's say I did an excellent job of summarizing, what do I need to do next?" The answer is: "Review."

What Happens When I Review?

Every time you recall information from memory, you activate the neural pathways to it. By reviewing regularly, you strengthen these pathways and improve your brain's ability to "fetch" or retrieve information. In this way, review minimizes forgetting.

When should I review information?

You have many opportunities to review before class and after class. It is a good habit to review in the morning when you wake up. You may also review while you are waiting for class to start.

See if you can remember the three or four most important points from the last lesson. Just close your eyes and try to remember what you learned in this subject the last time you had class. Focus on recalling the main points.

Then, look over your notes from the previous lesson. Verify that you remember the most important points. These are the points that you marked or highlighted when you summarized.

Reviewing before class provides a big benefit for learning. It helps your brain get ready to connect what you already know with new information in the upcoming lesson.

<u>What smart study habits can I use to review?</u>

You are able to remember things best when you space out your review over the days, weeks, and months after learning them.

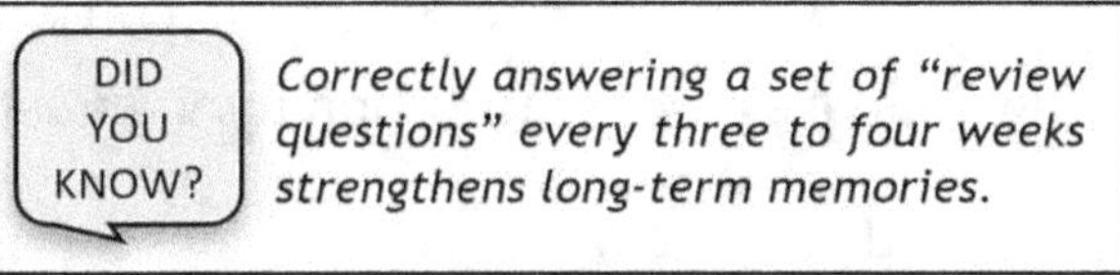

Throughout a semester or school year, you will want to refresh your memory as you update it with new knowledge. Plan on reviewing a lesson several times. For example, review it once per week for a month. For multiple classes, this may seem overwhelming without a realistic schedule. Plan out your available study time in twenty-minute sessions with sufficient stretch breaks to keep your blood circulating.

Around the globe, committed learners study for hours at a time. The weekends are perfect for reviewing what you learned in a subject during the week. If extra study time seems like a real challenge, then start with twenty minutes and work your way up to an hour or more. Do what you can to add study time into your weekend because it will improve your memory, save time, and reduce stress later.

<u>Creativity can help you remember what you learned</u>

To remember more of what you learn, make study time more interesting. Use creative methods and challenge yourself to remember what you learned. For example, you can create memory cues. The letters "S-E-W" can help you remember how to manage your attention during a lecture.

> S - Start with the main points.

> E – End with a summary of the main points.

> W – Write questions to help yourself focus during the middle of the lecture.

Another way to remember key points is to make up a story or use imagery. The story about the "Dust Bowl" illustrated that Mindy forgot the <u>middle</u> part of the lesson because she let her brain go into <u>down-time</u>. The imagery of the rollercoaster showed that down-time occurs in between peaks of prime-time at the beginning and end of a lecture.

You can use your creativity to make review more fun. For example, make a storyboard of the lesson using sticky notes on the wall (or a piece of poster board). Write a main point on each note, then post the notes in a logical way and review. Later, you can add more notes and display the "big picture" of what you have learned. Your display will allow you to see connections and have Aha! Moments.

Chapter 5 – Summary

Knowledge is power. Remembering what you learn is important for your success and growth as a learner. To remember what you learned, summarize, and review each lesson often. Also, take care of yourself and get enough sleep.

Twenty-four hours after a lesson you can only remember what your brain saved while you slept. Summarizing tells your brain what to save.

At the end of every lesson, invest about five minutes summarizing the main points. Otherwise, you should summarize before you go to sleep.

Review minimizes forgetting. By recalling what you know from memory you are re-activating the neural pathways to the information. Review on a regular basis so you can strengthen these pathways and improve your brain's ability to "fetch" information.

Over a period of days, weeks, and months, you will forget what you have learned if you do not review. It is critical to review often enough to remember what you have learned.

Review with the tools that work well for you. Be creative. To help you remember the most important information, use memory cues, story boards, and "how" & "why" questions. Using a "question and answer" format helps you remember vital information. For example, to review this chapter, go over these questions:

- Why summarize? When is the best time to summarize? How should I do this?
- Why review? How often should I review?

In our next chapter, we will share tips for paying attention like an expert.

6

Learn Like Experts

Aim, then shoot. Not the other way
around.

In this chapter, discover how experts can help you learn.

<u>Main Points:</u>

1. What can we learn from experts?
2. How does thinking like an expert help me learn?
3. How can questions help me learn?

New learners and experts pay attention differently. Experts see the big picture. Learners see separate details.

<u>What can we learn from experts?</u>

Experts, like your teacher, can help you sort out what is important from what is not. When your teacher shares the main points, capture them. Use them to organize the information.

The first time you learn about a topic, you begin with one part at a time. Using this approach, it takes a while to complete the picture. To see the whole picture sooner, focus on the main points and then, ask yourself, "How can I connect the new chunks of information with what I already know?"

Your teacher can help you do this because he has the "big picture". He knows the specific knowledge required for your subject and grade level.

Let's say you are taking a geography class. Your teacher recalls geography facts from memory and demonstrates how to use an atlas. He teaches you what you need to know to understand the basic geography of North America.

Imagine the same teacher as a student. Like you, he learned about the existence of land masses and identified continents. After learning how to use an atlas, he labelled maps with rivers and mountains. He faced similar challenges to yours.

Today, your teacher is an expert who helps you learn. He enjoys answering your questions, pointing out key features, and ensuring that you know your continents as well as how to use an atlas. By following his lead, listening, and completing the assignments you stand to gain a bit of expert wisdom. While the teacher's wisdom is available, you need to exercise skills to receive it.

Your teacher can help you sort out 'what is important' from 'what is trivial'. Ask questions to target what is most important.

<u>A Restaurant Story: The Menu, the Server, and You</u>
Let's say you go to a new restaurant. Your knowledge of the menu is based on what you have heard about the kinds of food the restaurant serves. The questions that you can ask the server will reveal your knowledge of the menu.

The server may ask what kinds of things you prefer to eat and identify similar menu items. He will describe the items that are most important to you. He does not go over every special or the entire menu of appetizers, drinks, and desserts.

With the information he provides, you are able to close the knowledge gap "just in time" to place your food order. What you learned from the server in this brief time period expanded your knowledge enough to place your order without becoming overwhelmed.

How does an expert help me learn?

An expert can identify the main points for you. In the restaurant example, the server provided the right information at the right time. Similarly, an expert teacher identifies your learning needs and helps you explore a "menu" of knowledge. Your teacher has a good idea of how to present the information in ways that are meaningful for you. He helps you make choices about what to pay most attention to as you learn in class.

Teachers, as our experts in the classroom, know what path to put you on based on what you already know. To ensure you are on the right track, ask yourself: "What are the main points? How will I know when I have mastered the lesson?"

A Drive-Thru Story: Ordering Fast Food with Dad

Now, it's your turn to play the expert. Think about everything on the menu at a popular fast food restaurant that you like to visit. This week Dad drives you there instead of Mom. Imagine your Dad pulling up to order food at the drive-thru. The menu is completely different from the last time he saw it. He has never ordered from this menu before. He does not know what to order. The menu board has a hundred items on it.

In this situation you are the fast food expert and Dad is the novice. Think of what you want him to order for the two of you. What are the most important things to order? What is the least complicated way to describe the order to Dad, so that he can place the order?

<u>How to provide an explanation</u>

When you explain something for the first time, focus on the most important points. Describe the main points without too many details. You have many ways to communicate the food order from the menu to Dad. Here are two: You could say I would like a number two meal with a bottle of water, and BBQ sauce; or, you could say each menu item separately in detail and drive him crazy.

As a fast food expert, your goal is to help your dad know what information requires his attention the most. This way you can ensure that he orders the correct items.

When you help your dad decide what to order for himself, you are like the server in the restaurant example. Think about what your dad likes, and what is the number of that meal on the menu? Maybe he likes what you do and then it is real easy! Either way, it pays to clearly state what to order so Dad learns that he may want to return to this fast food place with you again. Warning: Do not try to place a complicated order with a novice (e.g., grandpa). Smile.

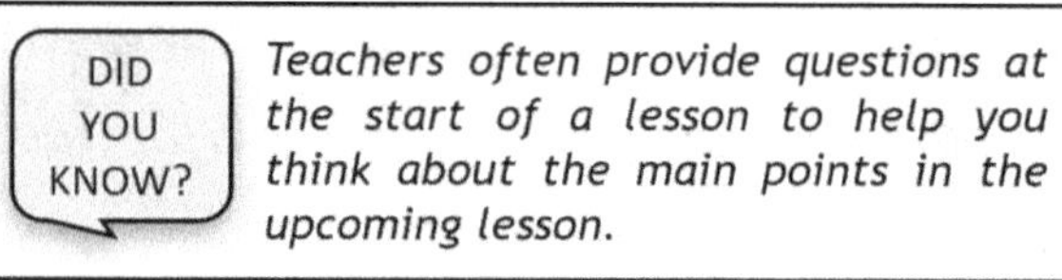

How can questions help me learn?

Pay close attention when your teacher provides a set of questions at the start of a lesson. These questions usually reveal the main points of the lesson. Read the questions to see what you know or do not know about the topic. As your teacher presents the lesson, listen for clues and make note of the answers to each of the questions that he gave you when the lesson began.

Questions are useful to learning because they spark your brain's natural curiosity. When your brain searches for answers, you may identify gaps in your knowledge. Pay attention to these areas so you can fill the gaps. Every time you fill a "gap" with valuable information, you experience an Aha! Moment.

Chapter 6 -Summary

All novice learners face a significant challenge, "What do I need to take away from this lesson?" Your teacher is an expert who can help you identify the most important points in each lesson.

Like a compass has points indicating North, South, East, and West, the lesson's main points provide you with a sense of direction. When you know the main points, you can pay attention intelligently and organize the information in ways that make sense.

When questions are used for learning, your brain searches for answers and identifies what you know as well as "gaps" in your knowledge. Great questions target the most important points and help you master the lesson.

In this chapter, we discussed how thinking like an expert helps you direct your attention to what is most important. In the next chapter, we help you take charge of your own learning.

7

Advocate for Your Own Learning

Stand up for yourself. Ask
questions. Listen. Learn.

This chapter equips you with skills to become an advocate for your own learning. Why struggle when you can take action to get better results?

Main points

1. What is an advocate?
2. Why should I be an advocate for my own learning? What's in it for me?
3. How do I advocate for my own learning?

What is an Advocate?

An advocate is a person who speaks up with a useful purpose in mind. Learning is your purpose. To support your learning, you can advocate for yourself by asking your teacher for help when you need it. This is OK for you to do. Both in class and in the days, weeks, or months after the lesson, it is your right and privilege as a student to ask for help.

As a student, it is a smart idea to review your notes from time to time. You owe it to yourself to fill in any knowledge gaps. Like a learning detective, do your own investigation to find answers to your questions. Show your teacher the answers that you found. Let her confirm that they are correct.

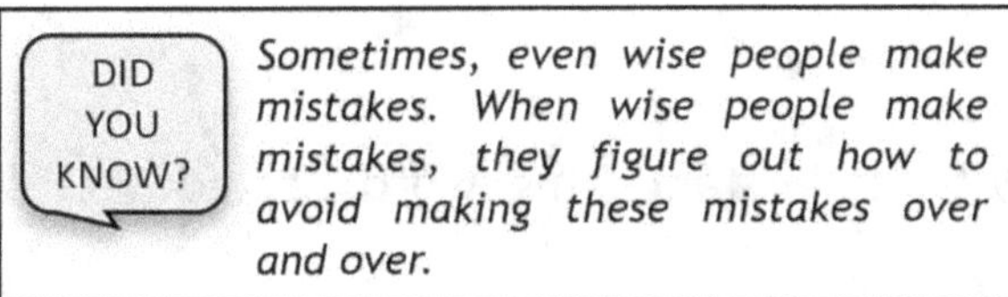

We all make mistakes

You can learn from your mistakes and stop repeating them. When it comes to detecting errors and learning, you need to be a problem solver. Think of your teacher as a resource who can help you find a solution.

You also need to be a communicator. If you are stuck after several thoughtful tries, ask your teacher for help. If you do not ask for help when your brain is ready to learn, the opportunity is missed.

Be an Advocate: Ask for Another Explanation

Your teacher has more than one way to explain things. When she explains things in a way that you do not understand, speak up for your own learning. Teachers like questions such as these:

"Could you please explain this to me in a different way?"

"Sorry, I didn't understand the example. Can we try another example?"

"I didn't understand this word, could you please simplify it for me?"

"I am having a hard time getting this but I want to learn, could you please show me again, how this works?"

Another way to communicate with your teacher is to say what you are thinking. You may say:

"Here is what I understand so far..., what am I missing?"

"I heard this... Is this what you mean?"

"When I get to this section, what happens is that I don't understand what to do next."

"If I show you my work, could you show me where I am going off track?"

Your teacher could say, "Here is the cause of the error. Try doing this before you do that." Your teacher's directions can help you to figure out a solution to your dilemma. When this happens, you have an Aha! Moment.

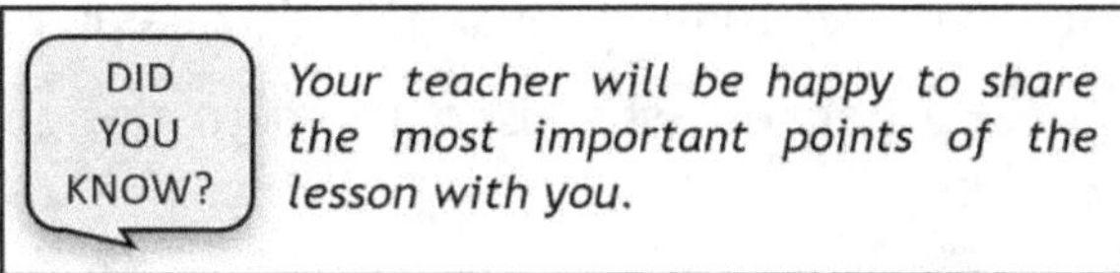

Be an Advocate: Find out the Main Points

Your teacher wants you to know the main points of the lesson. When you know the main points, you are better equipped to pay attention. The main points help you to connect pieces of information together and learn more effectively.

Not knowing the main points can cause confusion and problems for learning. Suppose you listened to forty minutes of lecture, heard dozens of facts, and still did not find out the main points of the lesson. How will you sort out the useful information? Without knowing the main points, you are unlikely to remember much of what was presented.

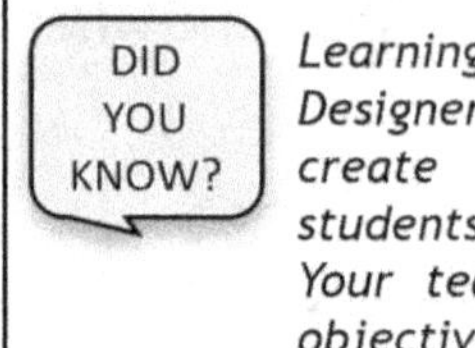

You have the smarts to learn the main points of every lesson. Therefore, feel comfortable asking: "What are our learning objectives for today's lesson?" Your teacher will have these handy because she used them to design your lesson.

Most teachers write the learning objectives for the lesson on the whiteboard or show it on a screen. When the objectives are not posted, ask your teacher for them. Asking about the objectives shows that you care about learning what she hopes to accomplish with you. Your teacher is likely to smile at your interest level.

<u>Be an Advocate: Understand Your Homework Instructions</u>

When you receive an assignment, take a moment to look over the instructions to see if you understand what you need to do. This is very important when you are assigned homework without practicing a few examples in class. Quickly review the directions to ensure that you understand how to do the homework. If you do not understand, ask your teacher to explain the instructions. When you request help, your teacher may share the explanation with the whole class so that everyone benefits.

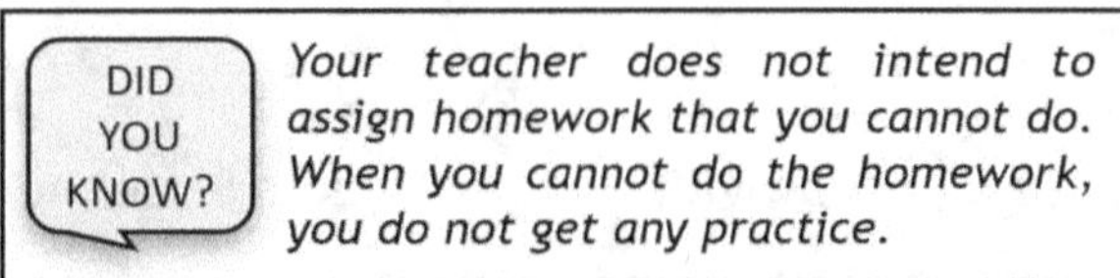

Your teacher provides homework to give you useful practice. In this way, homework helps you remember the lesson and boosts your confidence.

<u>Tips for Contacting Your Teacher Outside of Class</u>

Let's say that you run out of time to ask your teacher a question about the homework, what will you do? Maybe you could ask the teacher for an explanation via email. Find out how your teacher prefers to be contacted. Make it easy for your teacher to respond to your request.

Your teacher really wants to help you apply what you learned in the lesson, but do not wait until midnight to ask for assistance. It's not polite. Ask for help during normal waking hours and contact your teacher in the way she prefers to be contacted. Remember, your teacher needs time to respond. Annoying your teacher will not get you the results you want.

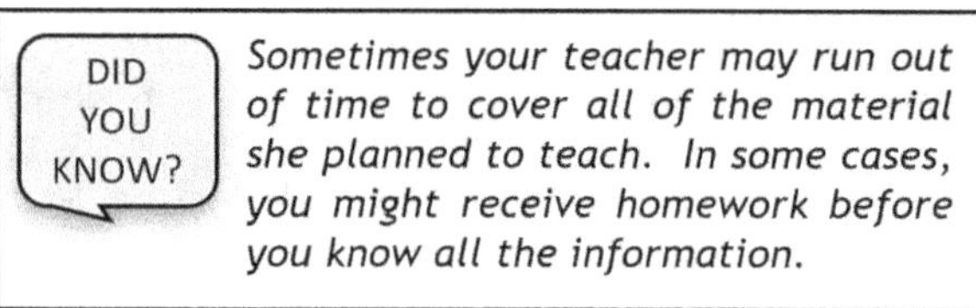

Be an Advocate: Understand Expectations

When your teacher provides big projects, you need to ensure that you understand her expectations. Here's how you can ask for more information:

> "Hi Miss, I want to understand your expectations for the project. Can you show me any projects that students have completed in the past?"

> "I want to earn an "A" on my presentation. Do you have examples or videos of great presentations from last year?"

Remember your teacher appreciates an eager to learn attitude. When you show that you want to learn and ask for specific information, your teacher is more likely to provide what you request.

How to Advocate for Your Own Learning

Here are important skills that you can master as an advocate for your own learning:

1. Ask questions when you do not understand an explanation.
2. Find out the most important points of the lesson and use this knowledge to ensure you pay attention to these points.
3. Look at your homework instructions while you are in class. Make sure you understand what you will need to do later when your teacher is not with you.
4. When you get assignments and projects, ensure that you understand your teacher's expectations.

Work on Your Own

When you have questions, start by trying to learn on your own. Transform into a learning detective. Think about what you are trying to learn, make a list of questions and scour your textbook and safe online resources to search for answers. This is a proven method for learning.

<u>Ask a Friend</u>

Usually there is someone in your class who understands the topic and can explain it in a way that you understand. Classmates can be good tutors because they see the lesson through the eyes of a student.

<u>What do I need to do before I approach my teacher?</u>

Try the question and give it your best effort. Show your work in writing and help her see where you are getting stuck. Then, she will be able to focus on helping you learn the correct reasoning.

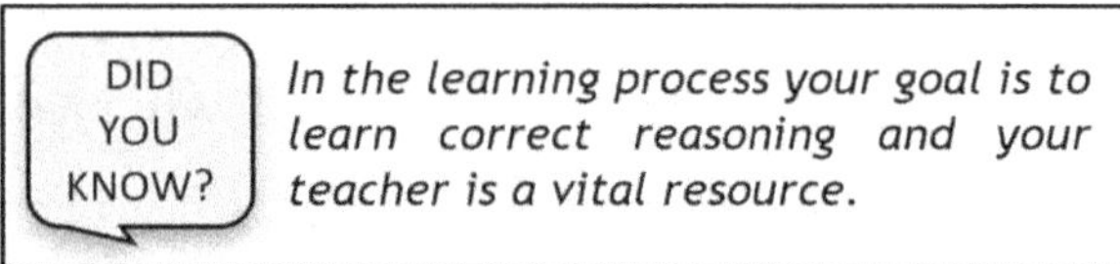

<u>Make Your Teacher Your Ally</u>

To be a strong advocate for your own learning, you need to make the best use of your resources. As far as possible, talk with your teacher because she is the expert. Your teacher's past experiences from teaching the same subject to many students makes her a good ally to have by your side. For you to benefit the most, it is best if both you and your teacher are advocates for your learning.

"Aha! Moments" happen when you are an advocate for your own learning and your teacher responds with clear explanations and feedback. So, take charge of your own learning by asking your teacher good questions.

> *Teachers are on a mission to help students learn. They chose this career because it aligns with their life's purpose.*

Help Your Teacher Achieve the Mission

Teachers want to help you learn because teaching is "who they are" and "what they do". They worked hard to become teachers because they find joy in helping others learn. Make it easy for teachers to spot you in class. Present yourself with an "I want to learn" attitude.

Tune in. To indicate that you are listening, have an alert posture and make eye contact. Keep your spine straight, your head up, and your arms resting on the desk where you are taking notes. This tells your teacher that you are interested in the lesson.

Participate in class. Use your voice in such a way that the teacher can hear you well, but please don't shout. Ask questions in a tone of voice that communicates a real interest in learning. Talk with your teacher like you would your grandma or grandpa, slowly and clearly. Be calm and respectful. Value what the teacher has to say.

Master the lesson. Ask questions to clarify what you do not understand. As your own best advocate, approach your teacher, show your work, and ask for feedback to master the correct reasoning.

It may be true that teachers are busy, but they are willing to answer questions that help students learn. If you find yourself struggling, walk into the classroom, ask a question, and find out how much your teacher really wants to help you learn.

Chapter 7 - Summary

Take charge of your learning. Feel good about speaking up for yourself and asking questions. Advocate on your own behalf because you are worth it. When you struggle with a question, be sure to ask your teacher for help.

Your teacher is a valuable ally who can help you learn and grow. Three keys that you may need from your teacher are the main points of the lesson, a different explanation, and clear instructions on homework. This is how you can master every lesson.

To be a good partner for learning, present yourself with alert body language, a clear speaking voice, and an intention to learn. Be prepared to show where you are stuck so your teacher can provide a helpful explanation.

After you master a topic, you experience feelings of accomplishment and confidence. At the same time, your teacher will experience the satisfaction of creating "Aha! Moments" with you. Years from now, you will have warm memories of the fun learning moments you had with your teacher. Make these memories ones that you want to remember.

In the next chapter, we will share how to become an intentional learner.

8

Be an Intentional Learner

Set new goals as you grow. Make
new choices. Grow your vision and
your plans.

Life is a classroom full of learning experiences. Imagine what you could do. Create a vision for the future that you want. Purposefully set goals, make a plan, and execute your plan. What happens next is up to you.

Learning holds the keys to a better life. When you are an intentional learner, you select what you want to learn with your goals in mind. Your choices are what makes your desired future a reality.

> **DID YOU KNOW?** *Your future life is built upon the choices you make today. Choose to grow every day.*

<u>Main points</u>

1. Imagine "anytime" in the future. What do you see yourself doing?
2. Right now, what are you doing to move in the direction of your goals?
3. What kinds of experiences, knowledge, skills, and attitudes will you need to create the life you imagine?

Write down your thoughts. Draw pictures of what you want your life to look like. Make a vision board with pictures of your desired future.

<u>Begin with the end in mind</u>

A famous author, Stephen Covey, wrote about the habits of highly effective people. One of the habits that he mentioned was that they "begin" whatever they do "with the end in mind." When it comes to your learning, begin with a specific goal and set a realistic timeline for yourself.

<u>Why is having goals important?</u>

Imagine life with no vision or goals. When you simply "play along" like a character in a movie, you play your role according to the script. Like a movie, events "happen" to you. Your life can be dramatic, boring, happy, sad, action-packed, or chaotic, and you react to the scenes.

In life, all of us are moving along, but some of us are choosing our goals, learning every day, and making changes to reach our goals. Take action to get the results you seek. Too many people say that what they do depends on the world around them. If you want results, then do not make excuses. Make <u>choices</u> based on who you are and what you value.

Set Your Own Direction

You can change the script and the settings of your life story. You have the power to direct the plot and develop the main character, "You." Let directing your future become the driving force behind the choices you make to educate yourself.

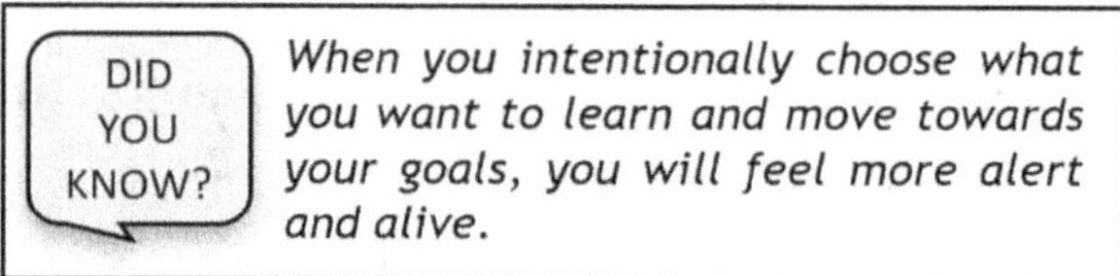

This change, from actor to director, will dramatically impact your life. New opportunities will arise as you choose interesting experiences and learn new skills.

Be an Intentional Learner

What is your greatest tool for building a future? It is your mind. Your mind is a tool that you must use with intention. Imagine the life that you want to create for yourself. Explore what you can do and forget about what you can't.

Once you become an intentional learner, it will seem dull to simply "play along" when you can "make choices" about what you will learn and do. There is no need to "act" like an "extra" who fills out the cast or reacts on cue. Your life can be full of meaningful "learning experiences" rather than a series of "circumstances" that dictate your attitude.

<u>The Planning Process and You</u>

Set goals and begin learning with the intention to reach them. For example, if you like cooking and want to be a chef, then you may envision yourself owning a signature restaurant, cooking for friends, or running a catering business. Each possibility requires special knowledge and skills.

Once you decide to follow your vision of owning a restaurant, you can set a goal of working in a few different restaurants until you graduate from college. As you gain experience, you will see how to run a business. You may think you want to open a French restaurant, but the market might prefer a "farm-to-table" theme. After doing some research, you can adjust your goals and plans to fulfill your vision.

To get started on a desirable pathway, picture your future career-life as clearly as you can. Be curious. Do research and make a list of what you need to learn.   Research includes interviewing someone who is doing your dream job. Make choices that take you where you want to go.

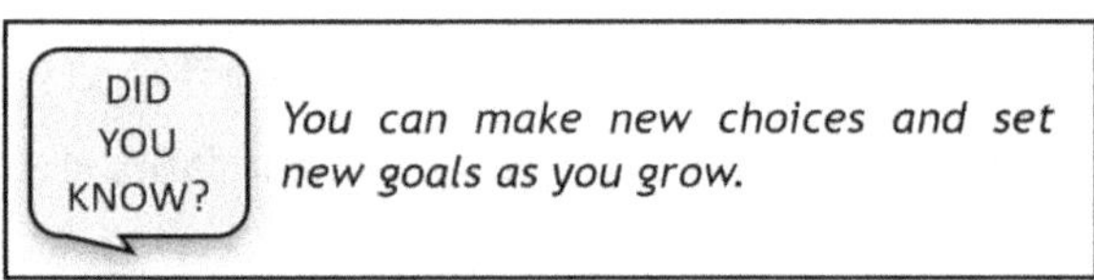

<u>Your Goals, Your Decisions</u>

Be aware that the goals you set now are not final. At each stage of your life, your goals move ahead of you, and you can change them based on new information, experiences, and opportunities.

As you travel along your life's journey, you will come upon forks in the road. At each fork, you will need to decide, "Will this path take me closer to my goal?"

It is helpful to look at positives and negatives when you are making choices. Using a blank sheet of paper, write the question at the top and draw a line down the middle. For example, the question might be: "Should I go to college?" OR "Should I buy a car?" Write the advantages of your decision on one side and the disadvantages on the other. As you consider the gains and losses, you will actually be doing a cost-benefit analysis. This will help you make a good decision.

Illustration of a Cost-Benefit Analysis.

<u>Should I buy a car?</u>

<u>Benefits</u>	<u>Costs</u>
Independence	Car payment
Drive to school	Insurance
No parents!	Gas
Give rides to	Pack my own
friends	snacks
	Miss my mom

The wheel of your future is in your hands. Pay attention to your choices and explore possibilities. Your goals will change as you age. Some of these changes will be as dramatic as the transformation of a caterpillar into a butterfly.

Just as it takes time and effort for the caterpillar to become a butterfly, your growth requires time and effort. Hold on to your vision and grow.

<u>Footsteps</u>

Seek trustworthy people to help you learn and grow. One of the best ways to learn is by following experts. Learn from their successes as well as their failures. You can learn from other people's mistakes even if they are not still alive today. And, you can do so without experiencing their pain, or losing the time and money that they did. Why repeat others' mistakes when you can learn from them?

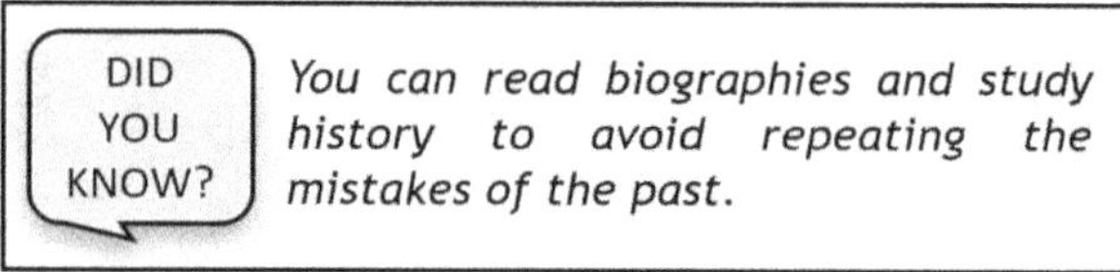

It is tempting to be a "follower" but at some point, you are going to have to make your own plans. As you look for the best path, select routes that help you travel towards your goals.

Chapter 8 – Summary

Use your vision to create a set of goals. Research how to attain them. Make a plan that you can follow to reach your goals.

As you work your plan, freely consider your options. For example, ask yourself "What if I could do this or that?" or think "If this happens, how will I respond"? These open-ended questions can help you make new plans for your future.

When you come to a fork in the road, take action to become the person you want to be. Choose the life that you want and create it!

In the next chapter, we share a story about how two teenagers made their choices when they came to forks in the road.

9

Journeys

"The only person you are destined
to be is the person you decide to
become." - Ralph Waldo Emerson

In this chapter we share the story of two teenagers, the choices they made, and how their decisions shaped their lives.

<u>Main points:</u>

1. What did Calvin and Jayden do to start their journeys?
2. How did the boys learn about their talents and abilities?
3. What will you do to start your journey?

In the upcoming story, observe how two students chose life experiences on their journeys, much like you will do to start your journey.

<u>A Story: The Sidewalk</u>

It's spring. Jayden walks to school with his cousin Calvin. For Jayden, the best part of the morning is feeling the sun and the freshness of the air on his face. He likes walking to school with Calvin because of his easy-going smile and quick pace.

Today, they talk about the end of the eighth grade and the future. Sensing that high school is the start of something new, Jayden wonders how he will spend his summer. As green leaves spread from branches overhead, the boys imagine life after high school. An uncharted world exists beyond the boundaries of their neighborhood and without warning Calvin announces that he plans to go to college one day.

"Where?" Jayden asks with curiosity.

"To college I said."

"Yeah, but where?"

"Somewhere in Michigan, a state school, where tuition is paid by the Kalamazoo Promise Scholarship." As usual Calvin's answer is immediate but a bit vague.

"And then what? What will you do with a college education?"

"Good question. I really don't know yet. How about you— do you have any plans?"

Calvin laughed a little because Jayden liked to make plans. He liked to make plans a lot.

"Well, I suppose college is a good deal," Jayden agreed.

He wondered to himself whether Calvin was going to college without a plan. Jayden wondered about his own future. He did not see the point of going to college without a plan. He concluded that college was a place for people who know what they wanted to go to college for.

Jayden kept his doubts to himself so as not to show his uncertainty. He agreed it was important to go to college. He wanted to appear confident and committed to a "good" idea. Many of the people he knew said college was the way to go. Also, Jayden wanted to keep things in common with Calvin who liked to talk about the future.

Jayden wanted to do something with his life. He just did not know what. What if he went to college? What if he flunked out? His head was spinning. Next year, Jayden will be in high school. He decides to study and earn good grades to prepare himself for college.

<u>Compare and Contrast</u>

Are the two boys alike? Of course, the two boys walking down the sidewalk together on their way to school share some similarities. They grew up together. They live the same neighborhood. They go to the same school. They are thinking about what to do after high school. Yet, they have different interests and motivations.

Jayden looks around and views the world as he sees it. Friends say Jayden is practical and down-to-earth. He loves to make plans. He wants to connect what he will do with a worthwhile outcome.

Calvin can imagine where he would like to be one day. He looks around with an eye for opportunities. Yet, he has not explored his college options fully. Calvin is imaginative. What he thinks is around the corner is always better than what is in front of him. Calvin sees himself going to college, meeting pretty girls, and choosing his major after he gets there.

Both young men are ready to consider what they will do once they are out of high school. On the sidewalk, as they near the school they have made decisions that will change their lives. Choosing whether or not to go to college is a big decision. Where they go, who they meet, what they do in college will determine their future. Around their neighborhood, they observe adults complaining of having less choices than when they were young. Some of them wish they had made different choices at the forks in the road.

<u>Summer Jobs</u>

Before school is out, Calvin gets a summer job. He tells Jayden he is going to work twenty hours a week with his uncle's landscaping service. He asks Jayden, "Would you like me to put a word in for you with my uncle? We could work at the same job."

"No thanks." Jayden did not want to do "yard work" no matter what Calvin's uncle called it. He felt sorry for rejecting Calvin's offer. Although he second-guessed himself, getting a "j-o-b" was not part of his summer plans. Then, he realized that he had a problem. He had planned on having fun all summer with friends. Now that Calvin had a job, what could he do?

<u>The Vet Clinic</u>

The first day of "no school" Jayden rode his bike around the neighborhood looking for something to do. He saw a sign, "Help Wanted", on the door leading into the vet clinic. Jayden stopped to consider working at the veterinary clinic. He smiled at the idea of working with people and animals all day, even if he had to clean cages. He would prefer to work indoors.

Jayden walks into the clinic. The receptionist welcomes him and asks if he would like to apply. "How did you know?" Jayden says.

"Well, you walked in without an animal. How would you like to start today?"

"That would be great!" says Jayden. He fills out an application, calls his mom, and begins working in the vet clinic right away. Mom was pleasantly surprised. Jayden can't wait to tell Calvin about his new job. He knows it is going to be interesting to work in the vet clinic. He texts the good news to Calvin.

"Congratulations!" Calvin texts back.

<u>The Fourth of July Holiday</u>

Taking a long break from animal clinics and lawn care, Jayden and Calvin meet over the Fourth of July holiday. They talk about their summer jobs. Jayden has learned what it takes to calm down people and animals who arrive at the clinic worried and anxious. He knows what foods different kinds of pets eat. He has observed animals' ailments and how fast they heal. Jayden talks excitedly about learning from everyone in the clinic. At home he has taken an interest in searching the internet for general knowledge about the types of animals that come in for check-ups or treatment.

Calvin doesn't express much interest in lawn care, but he enjoys a knack for fixing things. He surprised himself by repairing a broken lawn mower and then learning how to take care of most of his uncle's equipment—which continually broke the more it was used. It seems like working with a team agrees with Calvin as he shares good-natured stories, quips, and jokes from his job. He fits in well with "the crew" who call him "Doc" because he doctors the lawn mowers. The crew recognizes Calvin's mechanical aptitude and encourages him to go to trade school to become a machinist. He had not considered that career, nor trade school before trying out this summer job.

<u>What happened in Calvin's future?</u>

In the end Calvin took advantage of the Kalamazoo Promise Scholarship to go to trade school. He grew his belief in himself and learned from others who knew the way. He excelled at mechanical skills and enjoyed the "hands on" training. He was open to learning all that he could about how machines work. His fascination with machines and his learning experiences helped him to refine his choices. As an intentional learner, he excelled in trade school and became a successful small business owner.

<u>*Remember Calvin's summer lawn mowing gig?*</u>
He started working for his uncle and discovered that he enjoyed fixing things. When Calvin worked in the lawn care business, he also learned about customer satisfaction and teamwork. These skills were useful as he built his own business.

<u>Remember Jayden's job at the vet clinic?</u>
From working at the vet clinic Jayden recognized how important it was to treat each person kindly and earn their trust. Jayden discovered his gift for explaining things clearly. Because he enjoyed helping people learn, he chose to become a teacher.

<u>What happened in Jayden's future?</u>
Jayden became a middle school teacher. He woke up every day excited to help young ladies and gentlemen learn. He set high expectations and built strong bonds of trust with his students. Jayden encouraged students to learn about the world around them and apply what they knew. He helped them to be successful in school and in life. Jayden often quipped, "Your brain changes every time you learn something new!"

Chapter 9 - Summary

To begin planning for the future, think of what you might do. Create a vision for yourself. Discuss this vision with people that you trust, like friends, family, or teachers who want to help you. It is never too soon (or too late) to think about the future. Research different possibilities and gain experiences that help you learn about yourself. Use your interests, abilities, and motivations to propel yourself forward.

The story of Calvin and Jayden included three snapshots in time. On the way to school, the boys discussed the future. During the summer, they chose different work experiences. After attending trade school and college, Calvin and Jayden enjoyed their careers. Along their journeys, they each learned more about their abilities and the opportunities that they could create for themselves as "intentional learners".

After reading Chapters 8 and 9, how will you decide what to do at the forks in the road? Answer the following questions to get to know yourself better:

- What do I enjoy doing?
- What do I have a knack for doing well?
- How can I use my strengths to shape my future?
- What will I do when I need to make a big decision?

The decisions you make at each "fork in the road" are yours. Every time you choose a path, consider the vision you have for your future. It helps to note the "Advantages" and "Disadvantages" of a particular choice. At each fork in the road, take the path that brings about the best benefits for you and your loved ones. Most of all, advocate for your own learning, explore what you can do, and get going in the direction of your vision!

Closing Thoughts and Tips

What will you do?
Will you make a map and use it?

Congratulations, you made it this far!

As you reflect on what you have read in this book, get on with the doing. What will you do to improve as a learner? Many suggestions were offered, some of which fell into neat categories. For instance, when in class, you can apply the daily workout from Chapter 1.

Daily Workout for Learning

1. Tune in.

2. Participate.

3. Master the lesson.

These tips seem simple until you strive to master each lesson, every day. During a long lecture, you can see the attention slump coming, and it is hard to avoid. However, you can stay mentally alert by asking questions and keeping in tune with the speaker. Also, make note of the main points and tell your brain what to remember. Ask questions like: What did I learn? Why was it important? How will I remember it?

A golden opportunity for learning occurs when your teacher provides guided practice in class. In this situation, you are challenged and supported to ensure you master the lesson under your teacher's watchful eyes. Show your work so that your teacher can provide useful feedback.

Useful feedback contains the essential do's and don'ts for learning a particular lesson. When you receive feedback, make note of any "gaps", and learn how to correct the errors in your skills and reasoning.

Having a guide by your side is an advantage. We suggest that your teacher is your greatest ally for learning. As an expert, your teacher knows the subject matter, designed the lesson, and has taught different types of students.

When your teacher gives you a challenging workout, use your brainpower and apply what you just learned. Be prepared to show your work before asking for help. To remember what you learn, you need to exercise your brain so that the lesson is memorable.

Your status as a student makes you the best advocate for your own learning. Your teacher is on a mission to help you learn. As an advocate for your own learning you can ask for help and rely upon your teacher's assistance.

As a lifelong learner, keep yourself focused and interested in what matters to you. This is an extraordinary power. Brainpower. You can set goals, chart unexplored territory, and find new ways to apply what you have learned.

Take charge of your own learning. By becoming an intentional learner, you can achieve your goals and enjoy a life worth living.

"Education is not the learning of the facts, but the training of the mind to think."

- Albert Einstein

Aha! Moments Creator Hall of Fame

With a grateful heart, we'd like to share a way to recognize great teachers. We have created a Hall of Fame where you can honor your best teachers by thanking them for all they do!

Add your teacher to the Hall of Fame by going our website and sharing how your teacher has made a significant, positive impact on your life.

To nominate a teacher, please go to:

http://createahamoments.com/hall-of-fame/

Helpful Readings

Bhola, D. S, & Piel, M. L. (2020). Create aha! moments: Tips for teachers. Lincoln, NE: Psychometric Solutions.

Bransford, J. D. (2000). *How people learn: Brain, mind, experience, and school.* Washington, DC: National Academy Press.

Covey, S. (1989). The seven habits of highly effective people. New York, NY: Free Press.

Coyle, D. (2009). The talent code. New York, NY: Bantam Books.

Csikszentmihalyi, M. (1990). *Flow: The psychology of optimal experience.* New York, NY: Harper Perennial Modern Classics.

Gallimore, R., & Tharp, R. (2004). What a coach can teach a teacher, 1975-2004: Reflections and re-analysis of John Wooden's teaching practices. *The Sports Psychologist*, 18(2), 119-137.

Guskey, T. R. (2010). Lessons of mastery learning. *Educational leadership*, 68(2), 52.

Hattie, J. (2012). *Visible learning for teachers: Maximizing impact on learning.* New York, NY: Routledge.

Jabr, F. (2016): Q & A: Why a rested brain is more creative. *Scientific American.* Retrieved from https://www.scientificamerican.com/article/q-a-why-a-rested-brain-is-more-creative/

Jackson, R. R. (2009). Never work harder than your students & other principles of great teaching. Alexandria, VA: ASCD.

Kawashima, R. (2005). *Train your brain: 60 days to a better brain*. Teaneck, NJ: Kumon North America.

Maslow, A. (1962). *Toward a psychology of being*. Princeton: D. Van Nostrand Company.

McTighe, J. & Willis, J. (2019). *Understanding by design meets neuroscience*. Alexandria, VA: ASCD.

Pohl, M. (2000). *Learning to think, thinking to learn: Models and strategies to develop a classroom culture of thinking*. Australia: Hawker Brownlow Education.

Rath, T. (2013). *Eat, move, sleep*. Arlington, VA: Missionday.

Sousa, D. A. (2006). *How the brain learns (3rd ed.)*. Thousand Oaks, CA: Corwin Press.

Thalheimer, W. (2003). *The learning benefits of questions*. Retrieved from http://www.work-learning.com/ma/PP_WP003.asp

Tokuhama-Espinosa, T. (2014). *Making classrooms better: 50 practical applications of mind, brain, and educational science*. New York: Norton.

Tokuhama-Espinosa, T. (2018). *Neuromyths: Debunking false ideas about the brain*. New York, NY: W. W. Norton & Company.

Wiggins, G. P., & McTighe, J. (2005). *Understanding by design*. Alexandria, VA: ASCD.

www.ingramcontent.com/pod-product-compliance
Lightning Source LLC
Chambersburg PA
CBHW070819240726
48654CB00007B/403